ON LIFE, TIME AND OTHER THINGS

MADHURI KATTI

Made with ♥ on the Notion Press Platform
www.notionpress.com

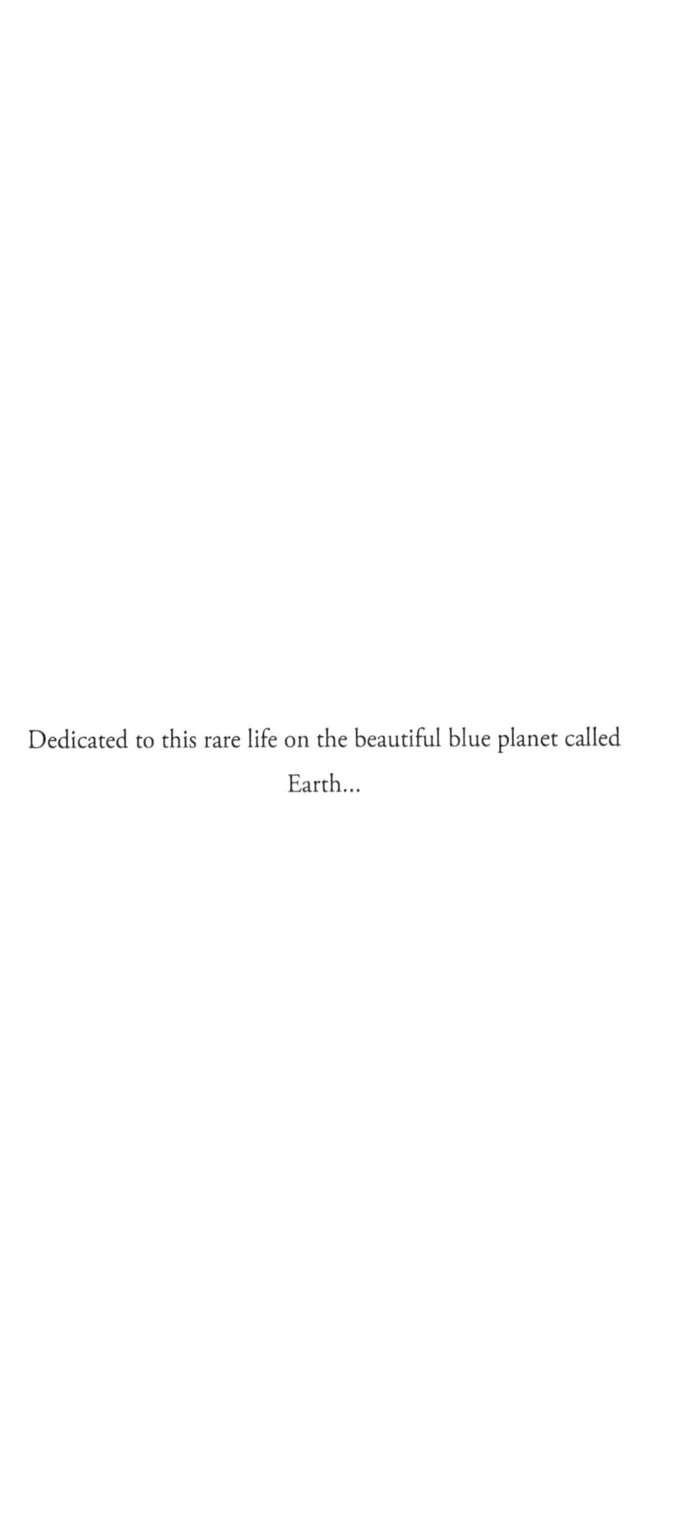

Dedicated to this rare life on the beautiful blue planet called
Earth...

Contents

Preface

I started writing poems since I was in middle school. Poetry came naturally to me when I was staring at a mountain near home and it never left me.

My first short poem which I wrote while staring at the mountain:

When we see shadows of a mountain

We are happy

But when we see shadows of a human mind

Are we Happy?

I really hope this compilation of my random musings on life, Time, conflicts and rest other random things which constitute life will find its own readers. I am just setting these poems, which were scribbled here and there, and later on my blog, free into the world as a collection with a hope that it will indulge readers who will spend a little time of their precious life reading my words.

Acknowledgements

I would like to acknowledge serendipities and coincidences which have always kept me going...

My Thoughts and My Words...

Chapter 1

Kaleidoscope

Escaping with little
Leaving home behind
A refugee in the world
Only a sky and courage to behold
Empty mansions
Tired caretakers
Only wealth to behold
A hostage to greed
Twain realities coexist
Yet they never meet
Peace is easy to violate
War remains difficult to negotiate
Ah! World…so predictable
With no new way ahead
We trudge the known bloody paths
Self-similar war games
Us and them
Power bereft of reason
Reason bereft of compassion
Compassion bereft of love

Love bereft of logic
Logic bereft of purpose
A farce called out
Wit bored of sarcasm
Futile cynicism
Kaleidoscope needs to be shaken
A new pattern must unfold
Out of all brokenness…
October 2023

A New Year

Yet another new year
Is back with the old baggage
Of fears and cautions
Prejudices and bigotry
Lurking shadows of
Diseases and death

They tell us
To hang on
To seek hope in
Science and prayers
Look for silver linings
And healings
Lost love
And musings

While prejudice kills peace,
And pride our compassion
While hate spreads
Like wildfire
Our comforts get
Traded and sold

While we lose our voice

And rights
Like Jesus
Or phoenix
Maybe they will rise
Just like balloons
Filled with their breath

Those little street urchins
They bear testimony of
Our collective failures,
Our naked emperors
Maybe their balloons display
Everyone's lost smiles!!
January 2022

A Rubble

It is easy to imagine
You are sipping
Your morning tea
On your favourite spot
Reading your book
And suddenly
It's all reduced
To rubbles
Except the place
Where you are sitting
In your favourite spot
You look for elevator
You need stairs
You need to run
Ground beneath feet
Did shake
And now it's just you
On a high rise
With roof blown
Staring in disbelief
Incredibly lucky? Isn't it?
To be perched precariously
To watch the scene change
Within seconds

You don't know

Is it a nightmare?

Where did this missile come from?

When did the war reach my home

Till yesterday I was a civilian

A honest tax paying citizen bystander

When I did I turn into a victim?

A witness to such horror?

Do they even know I am alive?

My dear and near ones who

Probably are watching TV

Sitting in their favourite spot

Will they count me among the dead?

With no signal, no electricity or kitchen

I will have to wait

With this rage, confusion

Fear and grief

Why were we abandoned?

Who abandoned us?

The governments? UN? God?

Will this attack bring peace?

Cease-fire atleast ?

Nations will spar

Deads will be numbered

And not named

Living ones will have no names

Only identities

Suspended in disbelief
I wonder if the house
Was it insured for missile attacks?
But was this an official attack?
Will there be a paper work?
How will they prove?
Everyone will spin the narratives
We are good in condemning
What we cannot prevent
Words, words and more words
Us and them
We forget – they made us
And we made them
Imagine, it is not too difficult
Planet on the brink of extinction
But till the end money needs to be made
Stocks to be bought and sold
No need to see what companies do
Buy and sell
As long as they bring in dividends
Was this missile made by you and me?
Play the probability game
The answer may be infinitesimal
But finite
Ofcourse we didn't know
Where our money went
Taxes and investments

We were just doing jobs
Building our homes
A place to be
With a favourite spot
To sit, sip and read
To plant our succulents
I look around
My spot, books, succulents
All are there
But rest all is destroyed
Reduced to a pile of concrete

They will find me and the dead
They need to mourn
And avenge!
October 2023

Time That Is Now

On somedays
I just wish to
Leave myself behind
Walking in some bookshop
Or in a forest
Or climbing a hill
Be someone with no plan
At a crossroad
On other days
I just race ahead
Trying to find myself
In unseen future
Maybe still
Walking into bookshop
Or being in a forest
Unable to climb that hill perhaps
But I just can't find or place myself
In the chaotic present
Where fear looms large
The past is receding faster
red shifting perhaps
And the future seems
To be taking forever to arrive
Maybe blue shifting on its way

Out of sync
Or perhaps out of breath
I glance back and ahead
Avoiding to look into the eye
Of the present that looms large
Will it devour us?
Time that is now
August 2023

Destiny and Luck

In the name of the
Sun and sky
Let me lament
For the lives
That derailed
One late evening
Just as their lives
Were chugging along
As ever, they were
Destiny's offspring
Unware that
That the game
Of destiny is
Forever fixed
Death is destiny
Life is luck
Suddenly many
Many lives
Ran out of luck
On that late
Summer evening
Destiny it is
To be born
In a land where
Apathy is normal
Kindness an anomaly

While their lives derailed
And were mutilated
Beyond recognition
In another far away land
Operation Hope
Was combing forests
To look for
Four lost kids
Their destiny
Lost game to Luck
June 2023

Storm

There bellows a strong wind
A storm arrives from strange lands
Just to irrevocably change
Everything that is and will be
Overnight it sweeps away
The cobwebs of Time
Changes the entire
Landscape of survival
There is no way to stop
The raging winds, tides
Lightning or the rains
No way to lock it all away
Change becomes eternal
Certainties uncertain
Life transforms
For better or worse
What remains same
Are dawns and the dusks
Motion of the planet
And yearnings of a heart
There is no going back
To recreate what it was
One that did not withstand
The winds and the storm

Yet condemned to hope
And dream
We sail our ships
Trusting oceans of Time
May 2023

Life and Death

Stink of death
Hits the nostril
Some poor creature
Took the plunge
Not realising perhaps
Its certain death

We can't see it
But stink is unbearable
More than the
Death itself perhaps
Of that pitiful creature
That was living

Life and living
Death and dying
Polar opposites
Starting and ending
Out of nowhere

An unbearable stink
An indelible mark
Life slips away
Just like that

Into the cloak of death

May 2023

Time

In vain
I try to hold
It back
But it slips away
Just like the cliched
Sand slips
Through the fingers
Time doesn't seem
Fluid or granular
But still
Behaves like one
Always flows away
Unidirectionally
Unintentionally
When I try to wrap it up
In my dreams
Or memories
I end up
On a mobius strip
No two ends meet
Beginnings don't
Always end
Endings don't seem
To have

Any beginnings
In a world obsessed
With origins and ends
Time plays a
spoilsport
It keeps winding
And unwinding
A perpetual clock
That keeps our
World dancing
On its rhythm
Of Tick tock
Tick tock!
April 2023

Love and Hate

Hate could
Learn lessons
From immortal
Love
How to hold
It all in
Till the
Heart breaks
How to turn
Away coldly
And never
Look back
You don't
Need a knife
Just words
Are enough
Hate could
Learn lessons
From Immortal
Immoral Love
How to
Let go
And not
Fight for

How to wait

Till it comes

To knock

On the door

Hate just

Wastes it all

By losing

The battles

For in wars

Hate just

Blinds you

Fools you

Love recognises

The other

Who stands

With the sword

Love knows

How to embrace

And defeat

All the hate

Hate just frets

Fumes and

Builds the rage

To go on rampage

Love remains

Immortal

Tiny cry of life

For Life itself
April 2023

Our Story

It is rather strange
How we get planted
In our own stories
Unintentionally

All characters
However likeable
Or unlikeable
Play their part

A hero
Could be an
An anti-hero
Or vice versa

Characters often
Become variable
Refusing to be
a constant

However chaotic
This drama of our life
We script it
Or it scripts us?

We get planted
Uprooted
Worshipped
And Cursed

For some we
Become breath
Toxic air
For others

Remembering
Forgetting
Othering
Dying

Ironically
We measure
Our lifetime
As Time and not Life
February 2023

Humanity

I see humanity cuddled on footpath
Dehydrated in summers
Shivering in winters
Tattered and battered
Seeking shelters
Oh, humanity, what a tender child
Staring with wide eyes!
Or at times a wrinkled face
With toothless grin
At times, a young girl
Bold and vulnerable
As we drive away
Avoiding the eye
And the sympathy
Humanity stares boldly
And walks away
We have our battles to wage
Days to face
And a future to create
Humanity has no place in it
We have learnt to look away
And Humanity?
Round the corner
Evil finds her and

scoops her in its arms
For it's victory dance
We did not save her
Yet we lament
Triumph of evil
And death of Humanity
Evil did not kill humanity
It was our collective apathy!
We clinged to our survival
While our soul was killed!
December 2022

Revisiting the Past

What looks like a wasteland
Exactly that's where
My home stood
With a beautiful garden
I stare at that land
That unsold dirty plot
Not belonging to anyone
Yet belonging to all
It was once upon a time
guarded by a tall wall
The wall is also half gone
While rest is totally erased
The land is covered with grass
The same grass we despised
But yet picked the holier ones
For the offerings
Along with the garden and home
My people and trees are gone too
I can almost hear the voices
Which lived there
How was it all demolished?
Brick by brick?
Blow by blow?
Or was it natural decadence?

I guess, I came looking for her
That barefooted wild girl
Who ran to school and cycled,
Played and giggled in the garden
As I turn around,
I find her on the wall graffiti
A barefooted wild girl
With her back turned upon the world
Strangely the roads
Where I learnt
To walk, run and cycle
Have remained the same
Just like the stubborn grass
Memories are stubborn too
So are some friendships
And roads we return to
November 2022

Journeys

Sometimes you know
At the end of journey
Either a new wound
Or a healing touch
Awaits you

Choice is yours
You can stay
With good old
Known scars
Or take the risk

You might return
With more scars
But the hope of healing
Always will fool you

You will jump into
The fire
With a hope of
Rising like a phoenix

Fools always
Dream of paradise

Only wise ones

Peer into

Dante's inferno

September 2022

Happiness on Discount

Have we become junkies
Addicted to hope and joys
Rainbows and silver linings
All things positive decoys?

We proclaim that
It is just
A matter of choice –
To be or not to be

How does it matter
If conflicts rage
Or forests go ablaze?

How does it matter
If someone is killed
Or incarcerated
For our rights?

They know
We enjoy cheap thrills
And discounted happiness
With easy EMIs on sale

How does it matter
If we are told to teach
Wrong facts or hate
Or fiction?

As long as happiness is
Prime and insta-delivered
Does it matter
If the planet is under threat?

They know we are junkies
Addicted to hope and joys
Rainbows and silver linings
All things positive decoys

Gambling away a future
We won't be a part of?
Doesn't it seem easy, quick
And affordable?
September 2022

Shame

Perhaps it is easy
To violate
A woman's body
And soul
And then walk with
Head held high
It is all done
To teach a lesson
To create fear

Perhaps it is easy
To plunder the earth
To dig out all
That is worth
And then walk with
Head held high
It is all done
For a profit
To create wealth

Will Earth save itself?
What about women?
Victims are silent
Our silence is more deafening

We will rage
For Earth, for Bilkis
Yet they will
Walk free
Reign free

That is how it is
Dont ask why?
It's reign of the
Shameless and inhuman
Emperor after all parades
In full nakedness and glory

How does one teach shame
To the shameless tyrants?
August 2022

Labyrinth

Trapped in the Labyrinth
It is often impossible
To get out the labyrinth
For the simple reason
You don't feel trapped
It doesn't seem what it is
You keep going onwards
While the labyrinth's design
Takes you backward
Blame it on the design
Or the divine
There is no way to know
That it is a trap
You go in circles
Thinking it's taking you forward
But it's a spiral descent
To nowhere or maybe hell
You are happy
With the clever deception
Who doesn't like
Illusion of happiness?
Who needs justice and peace
Happiness and prosperity?
The grand illusion of it all

Is fine enough
Why risk it all?
For which end?
It's an endless
Labyrinth
Fatigued, fogged
You are simply happy
Forward or backward or circles
How does it matter?
Soon lifetime will be served
Labyrinth will be inherited
Baton will be passed on
The game will go on…
Designers will blame the divine
Divine will be part of the design
Truth will become a beautiful lie
And all lies will seem truthful
It's an endless labyrinth
We need to navigate
To keep going
To reach nowhere or maybe hell
July 2022

The Blueprint

I see confident people
Who have figured it all out
Life's checklist and bucketlist
The job, insurance, taxes, savings
First home, second home
And a third getaway home
They know whom to hate
Whom to other, games to play
How to invent rules of the game
They cannot imagine
Someone's home being razed
Children being killed and maimed
Till the Chaos comes home
When their lives get disrupted
And the grand plan derails
Disasters seem to have a purpose
To reset and restore
Our hopes, dreams and ideals
I see people around me
Who seem to have figured it all out
Except for fixing, they know everything!
December 2024

Time Portal

On some days I wish
Time portal did exist
Just a familiar knock
Would lead me to its door
To another time, another space
More than the Time,
I miss the familiar spaces
With loving faces and embraces
That are forever lost
I wish to go back to a time
To enjoy long walks with my father
Have ice creams with my mother
Or to get into arguments
With my grandmother
about ungodly behaviour of gods
(While savouring her sweets)
I wish I could go back
To just be a naughty giggling
back-bencher in school
Or climb those Sahyadri hills yet again
To reach dilapidated fort premises
Just to lie on my back
Under open night dark sky
Beholding the starry night

Or maybe go back to a time
to be held
In a long tight embrace
by my very special little nephew
His eyes conveying fears
And a promise that
he would always
Be there to hold me tight
Wish he could return
Through that portal door
To me yet again
Sometimes dreams
become that portal
They take me back to time
That's when I wish
I don't wake up
To this hideous reality
Of an unsafe world
That teaches us
Only to doubt, fear and judge
I wish there existed a Time portal
And a familiar knock would lead me
To another world
Another time and space
Where I could be me
Throwing all cautions to the wind
Embracing or being embraced

By those I have forever lost
September 2021

Best not Taken

Thud – will that how it will sound?
Breaking lazy monotony
Of a rainy evening
Ensuing a chaos
Miraculously
Things will be taken care of
Strangers will curse,
blame and pity
And so will
family, friends and colleagues
People who never paused
To listen or understand
Will dissect your being
For hours
Gaslighting the departed
Absolving themselves of guilt
Everyone will move on
Within a day or two or years
Presence of a life will be erased
Unloved life would be lost in vain
Is that all there is?
Pause and look up
Behold the bird
Soaring in the sky

Flying into the setting sun
Birth is never a choice
But when death seems at times
The trick definitely is to
Keep breathing
Wait for the moment to pass
Look beyond
Outside your window
There is a life that awaits
That wants you to live
Take the pain in stride
And marinate your life with it
The last desperate step
Will definitely be
The best not taken!!
August 2021

Disbelief

We stare in disbelief
At life that slips away
Who knew just a breath
All that it takes to be alive
We stare in disbelief
At all the lives Washed ashore
Becoming nation's memories
We close our eyes in disbelief W
hen we cannot take it anymore
Confined in our safe homes
We turn into living ghosts
We stare in disbelief
As humanity fades away
We who love wars and winners
Are the tired vanquished lot
We stare in disbelief
As leaders trade away our lives
And our deaths
To build their empire of glory
May 2021

Dreams

I take long walks
In Latin quarters in Paris
I enter a random church
Someone is playing Ave Maria
I climb Sahyadri hills
Feeling free and fatigued
I walk along Marine drive
Watching rains approach
I am stranded in deluge
Waiting for a transport home
At times I am sailing
Along Tungabhadra in Hampi
Or I am listening to a stream
On some river bank in Bhutan
Or I walk and sob on a beach
Unsure of taste of salt
It could be sea
Or my tears At times
I am trapped
In Escherisque space
Or walking on a
Mobius strip
I am lost and then I am found
I reach yet I don't reach

While Uncertainty is
The only certainty
Waking hours
A prolonged nightmare
My escape and freedom
Is in my dream
Selfish it may seem
I don't want to be awake
I don't want to talk
Of nightmares today
May 2021

Just Like a Driftwood

Don't behold me
With contempt
Because I floated in
Just like a driftwood
I had a name
Born to someone
Isn't it enough
To qualify as a human?
Do not fear me
Do not hate my folks
Simply they couldn't afford
- Love, Pyre or a Grave
They probably thought
Water should be my grave
Instead of fire or earth
River being the river
Did what it does best
Buoyed me back
Just like a driftwood
I had love to give
But there were no takers
In the land of hate
River could have set me free
But it returned me to you

As a nameless corpse
To be counted among
The countless
River will remember me
Even if you don't
This beloved river is
Our memorial!
#CovidDeaths
May 2021

If Dead Could Speak

If dead could speak
I wonder what would they say
To every 'Rest in Peace'
They gasped for breath
They waited for beds
They trusted
They hoped
They left behind
Mounting sorrows
And bills
And plans
And dreams
They simply got erased
Without farewells
They got dumped
They got duped
Don't ever think
They are Resting in Peace
If dead could rise
From the ashes
And graves
And rivers
They would certainly
Rise in rage

May 2021

Waiting in the Dark

When will it be dawn?
I ask in desperation
Peering at the night sky
Stars too seem grim tonight

After the endless wait
There is a dim light
But, someone whispers
Hey, you missed the day!

What arrives is another dusk
Followed by the dark
Moonless night
Stars without their shine

Another endless wait
For the dawn
That never arrives
A dawn
That never arrives
April 2021

Heaven and Hell

Your idea of heaven
Is my idea of hell!
How will we ever reconcile?

You talk of supremacy
I walk with the oppressed
How do we find a middle ground?

You use brute loud force
I sing my songs of protest
Do you ever hear me?

You think might is right
I believe meek too has a right
How do I protect my child?

You are drunk on power
I root for my freedom
How do we avoid the fight?

Dice is definitely loaded
You will win this fight
But still you will lose

You will remember me
At the door of heaven
Your sins
Will be my testimony
Your lies
My truth

The fire you lit to hide your crimes
Will burn down the heaven
Your supremacy is a sham
You have power that is not yours

One day humanity will rise
One day humanity has to rise!
October 2020

Time

Sometimes I wonder
whether I lose track of time
or time loses track of me
Forgotten, erased, demonised
I lurk like the dark shadow
Waiting for the spotlight
To reveal that I exist
July 2020

Future

Fear looms large
Blurring both past
And future
Will we make it?
Random memories
Of a crowded bazar
Hot breakfast
A long trek
Memory of a comet
And night sky
Some dance steps
Old poem
All years melted
Away into tears
Music and laughter
Good friends
Gentle love
All locked away
Keys lost
Fear looms large
Palpable and real
But hey
Learn to look beyond
Seek beauty

And dreams
So many more
Moments yet to be lived
So many miles
Yet to be walked
There will be a future
A brand new one
Just like a new leaf
A place without fear
Just breathe in
And hang on….
July 2020

Storm and Me

The storm has abated
It did what it could
Shattered my existence
Where do I begin?
How do I pick these pieces?
There is no ground
Under the feet
It's all water
The roof over my head
Has blown off
Whatever I held close
Simply floated away
Some with water
Other with the wind
How do I get my life back?
How do I prove I am me?
How do I show?
Where my mud house stood?

It's all gone
Either with water
Or with the wind
Did you hear howling winds?
Did you see the waves rise?

Those uprooted trees?
My uprooted life?
No, you wouldn't notice
You were all locked in
Blind and deaf
Till they cleared it all
There is no sign left
Of howling winds
Of broken homes
Of my lost past
I too ask
Am I me?
#cycloneamphan
May 2020

Spin

What kind of a spin is it?

What goes around, does come around

Yet, its never the same!

Laws teach nothing is lost

Yet, much cannot be retrieved

The top is also below

A walk on the mobius strip

In a world so self-similar

Nothing is familiar

For – What is, is never,

What really it is!

What we know, is actually,

Only the depth of the unknown

And that bond also decides the drift

Stuck on a blue planet in a vast abyss

Where war literally is sold as peace

I wonder,

What kind of a spin is it?

March 2020

Lost Humanity

Scavenging under the rubbles
She looked for humanity
It was yet another day of
Strategic bombing

They tried to flee in vain
From guns and grenades
And bombs
And landmines
And beastly men

Death was everywhere
In every form
It caught up with all
Even those who escaped these
Troubled shores

She kept scavenging for humanity
Under the rubbles
Of the wasteland
Many died
For the sake of few
Who wanted to live

It was a lost battle
Under the rubbles
She scavenged
For dead humanity
February 2020

The Blue Door

There is a blue door at end of the road. People say it is the door to the happiness. One can hear laughter and songs, but no one is ever seen crossing the threshold. Neighborhood believes that all the peace and happiness has got locked behind the blue door. No one knows who has locked all the joys away but the sadness and anger that is left behind is quite palpable. As one walks down the road, one can hear screams of the locked lunatic siblings coming from an attic of one house. They say he lost his mind over a girl who was forced to marry someone from her clan. From another house one can hear heart rending lament of a mother whose only child has gone missing. A misogynist cop rants and screams in the other one, ordering his wife and children who tremble with fear. A young girl screams hysterically in the next one whenever she hears a footstep, "They are coming for me. Save me."

The town has a church, a temple, a synagogue and a mosque where prayers are held daily. Everyone prays for peace and prosperity that they think is locked elsewhere behind the Blue door. They all hold each other's faith in doubt. They all live in constant fear and pride of their gods. They fight and attack each other relentlessly. It feels as though they are compelling their gods to compete in a race to gain the highest glory and power of the land (just like they wanted the children to compete once upon a time). Sadly, they have managed to drive both gods and children away.

After prayers everyone returns to the little hell they have managed to create. The Blue door remains shut forever. In their fight, hatred and bigotry, the town has forgotten that the gods have left key to the door with them – the key that opens only when there is love and kinship.

November 2019

Howling Winds

It was in the news
Cyclonic storm was on its way
They did what they could
To prevent the disaster
They monitored the eye and the tail
There it was circulating,
feeding on winds
And gathering momentum
It all seemed calm on the shores
Till the waves began to move faster
It came closer,
Sounds of the howling winds
Made it all real
Everyone knew
All preparations were made
All estimates looked good
But there was no way to assess
The damage it did
Young ones quivered in fear
Homeless knew they will be
Unaccounted ones
Lonely man walked on the street
Unaware of the perils
No one had told him to be safe

He took shelter under the very tree
That crushed him minutes later
Howling winds
Harbingers of death
Preyed on lonely, helpless
And homeless
Farmers lamented as
Entire harvest got washed away
No one realised
Storm was our harvest
By feeding Earth, wind and seas
Our anger, disgust, greed,
wastes, pollutants and hatred
Cyclonic storm just churned it all around
And returned what we had reaped
With anger and vengeance
Winds, earth and sea turned hostile
Howling winds perhaps were warning us –
"Don't be a bully
It can all boomerang badly!! "
November 2019

Silence and the Darkness

When silence becomes deafening
And the words hide in the dark
Slowing erasing history
I try to figure out their forms
Or meaning or language
Nothing emerges
It's a dark dense space
Nothing is visible
Nor is audible
I wait
Maybe words are being born
Maybe a new reality is taking a form
What if it's a monster that's in the making?
What if the silence is made of inaudible screams?
As the world looks away in faith
Blinded by the festive lights
I will hang on to my doubts
I shall still try to listen to sounds of silence
And try to peer into dark abyss
With or without hope
October 2019

Jump

Unable to find answers
Unable to bear the questions
Acutely aware
Of all closed doors
And humiliations
And all silences
She decided to jump
As she walked along the edge
Too many thoughts
Crowded her mind
She wanted to cut loose
From the past
From the present
The questions
The helplessness
The despair
Her luckless and
Loveless life
When no one pays heed
When life is cruel
What's the point?
What's the point?
On and on
The thoughts fogged her mind

Tears blinded her vision
Suddenly a stranger stopped her
"Please take one bunch please.
I haven't eaten whole day"
A blur of bunch of yellow roses
Were staring at her face
Prodding her was
Another voice of despair
Carrying a bunch of bloom
What an irony!!
She paid the boy
And watched the train go by
She brought home
The yellow flowers.
She wondered…
There is a point maybe…
There are people maybe…
There are doors maybe…
There are paths maybe…
There is a future maybe…
That day she didn't jump
But took a leap of faith instead!
September 2019

Chain of Liberation

You ask "Why don't you dance with joy?"
There have been infinite invisible chains around my feet
I never knew that I was to undo them one by one
I kept them all 'as gifts'
I waited for some loving hands to undo them
I didn't know I have to undo them myself
One day you came along
And laughed at me…
You reached down my feet
But ended up adding one more chain
Now I struggle to undo them
Only one of them can't be undone
I call it the 'chain of liberation'
Which you gave me as a farewell gift!!!
August 2019

Bare Foot Joy

Making, flying and chasing paper kites
Bare foot
Running across the crowded streets
They seem to soar just like the kites
Kite runners look happy
Across continents their joy is same
For the moment
They are free just like their kites
Riding on the lightness of the moment
They behold pure joy
The joy that eludes
The boy across the street
Sitting in the car
Staring through the glass window
He is a prisoner of luxuries
While poverty has set others free
They run like wind
Through narrow lanes
They hop across building roof tops
While the other stays glued
To the smart phone screen
Sun kissed
Blessed by the evening breeze
Our kite runners seize the moment!

Ah! the bare foot joy
That eludes the little boy!
July 2019

Strange

Strange is the light that blinds
Strange is the light behind dark shadows
Strange is the joy that inflicts pain
Strange is the love that teaches to hate
Strange is the life that must end in death
Strange is the meaning that is absurd
Strange are the dreams that cannot be real
Strange is the reality that is a dream
Strange are the clouds that don't bring rain
Strange is the regret that hides the pride
Strange are the journeys that never end
Strange are the words that defy the form
Strange are the doors that never open
Strange is the religion that robs the faith
Strange are the bridges that separate
Strange is the war that is fought for peace
Strange are the journeys that never end!
July 2019

The Storm

Light breeze kissing the leaves
Dancing waves touching the shore
Whisper to me
Maybe a storm is on its way…
I want to be silent
I do not want to burden the wind
For my words might trigger a bigger storm
I wait silently for the storm to pass
Once again I shall be ready
To throw my words to the winds!
December 1999

Juxtaposed

Man against man
Man against women
Women against women
Man against Nature
You against me
All of us are juxtaposed!
One defines other
One ends other
One begins other
On a dark night
We seek light
On a sunny day
We look for shade
Light and dark
Day and night
Love and war
Life and death
Juxtaposed!
Sad seeks joy
Happiness
Sadness
Juxtaposed!
Broken against
The Whole

Nothing can stand
On its own
It needs the other!!
You eliminate one
Other loses meaning
Yet the fight remains
Eternal!
Juxtaposed
One belittling the other
Forever!!
July 2019

Old Ports

They hide tales
Old Ports
The getaways
Or the anchors
They have stories
About ships which sailed
And ones which wrecked
June 2019

Seeking the Moon

I seek the moon tonight
With thousands of others
From my window
Caged momentarily tonight
In my cell window
Moon too looks desolate
And Persecuted
Was I persecuted for
Beholding the Moon?
My parents at my faraway home
Me, at my detention centre
Along thousands of refugees,
Illegal immigrants
And activists around the world
All are looking at the Moon
Moon smiles as ever grimly
Bonded forever to the Earth
Spinning with twined destiny
It tells me
We all need to wait
There is no easy way
To Salvation
And Freedom
June 2019

Other

Peasants will rise
They will sing
They will protest
They will take bullet
They will save democracy
While we will fret
And intellectualize!
Educated middle classes
Don't you worry
These whom you 'other'
Will save your jobs too
They don't need you
But you do
To reap crops,
Cook your food
Cobble your shoes
Tailor your clothes,
Build your homes
Clean your homes
Toilets and cars too!!
After the revolution
They will still come
And assume their lowly jobs
While you will rot in your guilt

Or die with a foolish smug!
History textbooks will talk of them
But you will be mentioned
As the 'other'
-Who let the system down!!
#saynotohate
May 2019

Time

Time is wrapped
We move forward
But yet in circles
A new beginning
Another New Year
All dots
On the circles
Time is a trap
An endless wrap
Moving forward
Yet in circles
Histories repeat
Dictators return
But tyrant
Time
Beats them all
Let us not despair
No one colour or
One faith can
Rule Forever
Light refracts
Even through
The Prism of Religion
Into a Rainbow

All mighty forever
Will bite the dust
As children of soil
Will rise yet again
Time goes in circles
Some look ahead
Forgetting the wrap
Others who look behind
Fall in the trap
There is no way
Back into the womb
Only death awaits
Ahead
Time moves forward
While moving in circles
Maybe Sisyphus is happy
For he knows
The clock ticks…
April 2019

Strange Imprints

As the night falls

I wonder what

Set the pace

Of Time

It moves

Freezes

Goes back

And forth

Yet always

Arrow of Time

Points always

Ahead

It circles

Around the

Life and Death

Beginning

And the End

I look at the stars

I look back

Millions of years

Wonder how do they

See our history

Unfolding

On a tiny

Blue Dot
Strange is the
Arrow of Time
Pointing into
Nowhere
Ticking away
Turning
Itself into ashes
Rising like a phoenix
Yet it always
Moves ahead
Stubbornly ahead
Leaving behind
Strange mute imprints
A sand dune there
Or a mountain here…
February 2019

Staying Relevant

Staying relevant
In irrelevant times
Is the challenge
Engage
Or disengage?
Stay attached?
Or be detached?
When Time sweeps
You away from the frame
Should one linger
On the fringes?
Where does one go?
Is there a Rumi's field?
The even playing field?
Where they play it fair
No time to call a foul
A foul
No ground rules
It's a game
Where no one wins
But all try to
Reinvent
Shifting positions
Moving goal-posts

To stay relevant
In these irrelevant times…
February 2019

Silly Significance

With her chin-up
And chips down
With spring in her feet
She trots on the globe
Our blue dot
But she is not alone
There are billions of us
Totally lost
In the humongous mess
Of hundreds of imagined worlds
And faiths
And the great sense of propriety
All trying to be right
By proving others wrong
Kudos to us for
Throwing out the baby
– our sustenance
Along with the bath water
All self similar beings
Trying so hard
To advance their race
By killing each other
The sheer madness

We still love to imagine
And believe
It's the sun that sets
Or rises for us
Instead of –
– that's it's we go
Around an axis
Downside up
And upside down
Along the elliptical
Planet doesn't care
Whether it's dinosaurs
Or only us
Neither does the Universe
Feeling all self-important
With bloated
or deflated egos
With the chin up
Or chips down
We continue to seek
our significance
In the grand cosmic
Insignificance
But does it have all to be
So dangerously silly?
by pitting imagined worlds
Imagined selves

And imagined gods
Against each other
And against Nature!
January 2019

On Patriarchy

She tells
People ignore
Ah, the 'Drama'
He confesses
People dismiss
Oh, the 'Dark Side'
Ah, patriarchy
the dark drama!!
#metoo #patriarchy
October 2018

Blue and Red

They both argued
About glory
Red being red
Flaunted being important
Underlined with Red
Called Blue
The scatter brain
Blue being blue
Mellow in being
Simply said
I make most of my
Wavelength
And let small particles
Scatter me to the Oblivion
Thus played out
The most spectacular sunset
Blue sky smeared
with Vermillion red
Sun smiled as it set
Ah! the usual fight
Forgetting they
Both came from white light!
October 2018

Strangeness

In a strange city
Trees grow
In abandoned homes
And uprooted people
Dwell beside the roads
There is no place
To plant trees
There is no home
For migrants
Trees grow
Inside old homes
And people grow old
Without homes
Both trees and people
Have become refugees
And homes are empty
Devoid of love
And compassion
Trees and people
Search for roots
In a strange city
On a strange planet
September 2018

Here She Lies…

Under the Canopy

Here She lies

In Paris

In exile

At Pere Lachaise

A mother, a queen

With a vanquished dream

She crossed seven seas

A sin in the 1850s

In the hope of justice and freedom

From the Queen of England

Mocked, ignored and bribed

She told them

They could not own

The kingdom of her son

And her pride

Here she lies

Our own Queen of Oudh

Next to a bush of roses

Growing in the wild

In exile

at Pere Lachaise

Resting quietly among the greats

She sought nothing

But Peace and Freedom
Among all the shiny graves
If you see an earthly grave
Fractured by Time
Under a green canopy
Know that it's her
India's brave Queen Mother –
Janab-e-Aliah Mallika Kishwar
Who crossed seven seas
A sin in the 1850s
To seek Peace and Freedom
And fair political justice
From the Imperial queen
And did no compromise
Do pause
And pray
If you may
But do tell her tale
Here She lies…
In Pere Lachaise
September 2018

Kafkaesque

I exist therefore I am
I am therefore I exist
I am the means
and the end
I think
so I do
I do
so I think
I stand
so I believe
I believe
so I stand
I reason
to be
not to be
I protest
for Justice
That is blind
I am free
but chained
by law
But the law exists
to free the chains
what is Right

is also Left of Right
But Right cannot be wrong
so Left is definitely right
August 2018

Looking Back

History stares at me
Full of tales
From different eras
From different perspectives
A walk
Back in Time
To re-build the Time
To know the present
To shape the future
That's what Astronomers
Do as well
Look back in Time
To connect the cause
and the effect
In a chaos that reigns
August 2018

By the Brook

There she lay

In a lonely grave

By the Brook

Unseen and unknown

Till a lonely shepherd

Stumbled upon her

And found her tale

A glorious tale of

Love and loss

Of a royal Princess

The most beautiful

Tormented soul

Soon the stories

Were made

And unmade

Shepherd loved

The dead dame

And his fame

He tended to

The tomb

Soon lovers came

To be blessed

By the cursed Princess

Little did anyone know

Six feet under

Was a sad refugee

Who had lived,

In pain,

Loved,

And died in vain

Little did she know

Her death will give

Her a life, care

And a fame

And not far away

In the grand Cemetery

In an unmarked grave

Was the real Princess

Finally dethroned by Time

August 2018

The Day Freedom Was Won (and Lost)

They both stood vigil

Just like lovers

With surgical precision

Lines were drawn

And lives got thrown

Into disarray

One thought Nation did not belong to them

Other was too young and weak to claim or protect

The two great lovers

Stood and watched

As a Nation got ripped into two

And precious lives ebbed away

No one realised

It was the very idea of love and freedom

They had aborted that day

As the Nation bled

Along with lives

Homes

Identities

Peace

Love

Humanity

All was lost

And alleged lovers stood vigil

Arrogantly announcing

Their Nation's

Tryst with destiny!!

August 2018

Immigrant

They tell me I don't belong
To this part of the land
Under this part of the sky
On this shore
They tell me move back
But I came here
When they told me
I don't belong there
I was a refugee then
An illegal immigrant now
How many names will you give
To your own creations?
The divide that you created
The line that fractured the land
Into here and there
Us and them
You and me
I will go away…
History will repeat
I will move on
Move back
Move away
But when will you learn?
The Earth, Sea and Sky have no boundaries

Your mind has made it all up!
The imbecile mind
Which is addicted to war games!
I will outlive your games
Tomorrow you will celebrate my survival
You will share it million times
Just like war
You are addicted to stories
To social media
To internet
Between the persecution
And celebration
Millions will disappear
Lives will be lost
Many changed forever!
In this world of imbeciles
I'd rather be an immigrant!
I'd rather not belong!
Your riches
Will be forever indebted to my poverty!
July 2018

Emerging from the Dark

Engulfed by the light
Blinded
By own luminous being
Unable to see or feel
How others feel…
An era of knowledge
Bereft of Wisdom
Desensitized
Sensitivity reigns
A world
where refugee children
Face trials
Four year olds
Die smothered with lust
Hope is a lost cause
Let darkness descend
Light has led us nowhere
Maybe answers we seek
Lie in darkness
Let there be dark
And quiet healing
While emerging from the dark
Maybe we will learn to behold Beauty
And the Truth yet again!

July 2018

Lost Home

A realm of nostalgia
And melancholia
Lost in Time
And Space
Etched in memory
Laughter
Joys
Despair
A hearty meal
A good sleep
Warm cuddle
Siesta story
Playful kittens
Chasing their own tails
Naughty childhood
Trees in backyard
To climb and hide
And a bicycle to ride
Lost in space
And Time
A home
Unreachable
Home
July 2018

War

Canvas of history
Forever painted in red
Shows us the right mirror
Mankind has never been kind
Battle after battle
Peace has been butchered
Yet we dream and hope white dove
Will save us
Love will bail humanity
Even in garb of peace
We know to fight our
Cold wars
Power wars
Without weapons
Even between you and me
We identify the Other
To keep the fight on
We need victims
To feel the power
Even if we don't butcher
We bully in good humor
To eliminate the Other
Upmanship may drown us
Yet we steer our ships with pride

Towards annihilation and regret
Metaphorical Phoenix
Rises from the ashes
But we keep the embers burning
To start the next war
With every hope demolished
Love turns into a refugee
June 2018

Brokenness

Brokenness
Sometimes I wonder,
Is it the brokenness
which holds the world together?
a crack that still holds parts?
Is it the brokenness that
unveils the Whole?
The imagined whole –
That never will be or
Maybe never was…
Even if the cracks give away –
Can broken pieces be
whole parts in themselves?
Or maybe broken parts
Will create a kaleidoscope
Sometimes I wonder
Is it the brokenness
that holds the world together?
What purpose does the Whole serve?
The Whole which excludes,
smugly nestled in itself
Till a crack breaks the egoistic shell
The Whole will never be a whole

Sometimes I wonder,

Is it the brokenness that

holds the world together?

Borders divide land and humans

But yet, when challenged

The humanity that rises,

Is often more than the sum

Of the broken souls

Sometimes I wonder,

Is it the brokenness that

that holds the world together?

June 2018

To Gabo, With Love

When life turns mundane
And days repeat themselves
When people and their acts
Seem self-similar
I think of you, Gabo
I wait patiently
For magic to spring from reality
It does spring from Life
From the mundane
On dullest day
I step out to behold
The beautiful spring
A saddest day
Holds a surprise
Dreams I dare not
Yet they come true
The places I got kicked
Same places do spring tickles
Instead of me seeking beauty
Beauty seeks me
When the world tells me I am wrong
I wait in the dark hour
For the light and truth to appear
To liberate me

Gabo, thanks for teaching me
Teaching me to wait
To look for beauty in the decadence
To see life and hope spring
From unusual dark spaces
Thanks for bringing to us
The tale of Ship-Wrecked Sailor
And the woman who trained her dog
Trained it to visit her grave
For Hundred Years of Solitude
And Love at the Time of Cholera
For teaching me Love and Death
Mean the same
Thanks, dear Gabo
March 2018

Legacy

I stand tall
In the pages of history
And in city landmarks
You cannot ignore me
Because I thrive
Because I survive
Despite all odds
I linger
As a citadel
A memorial
A grave
Marking my presence
In Space and Time
You cannot
Wipe me
Forget me
Abhor me
Hate me
Because I tell a story
Of the Times gone by
Of our entwined histories
February 2018

Palace of Dreams

The Palace of Dreams
Lies in Ruins
Entangled in roots
With growing shoots
Stands a colossal memoir
Of the Time that was
And that never will be…
February 2018

Humanity

Humanity
I see humanity cuddled on footpath
Dehydrated in summers
Shivering in winters
Tattered and battered
Seeking shelters
Oh, humanity, what a tender child
Staring with wide eyes!
Or at times a wrinkled face
With toothless grin
At times, a young girl
Bold and vulnerable
As we drive away
Avoiding the eye
And the sympathy
Humanity stares boldly
And walks away
We have our battles to wage
Days to face
And a future to create
Humanity has no place in it
We have learnt to look away
And Humanity?
Round the corner

Evil finds her and
scoops her in its arms
For it's victory dance
We did not save her
Yet we lament
Triumph of evil
And death of Humanity
Evil did not kill humanity
It was our collective apathy!
We held on to our survival
While our soul was killed!
December 2017

City Records

New names added as
Properties change hands
Belonging to none
Land gets title
Gets owned and disowned
Dusty city records
Become testimonials
Of passage of Time and People
July 2013

Life goes on...so do my musings, ponderings...just like a river I meander aimlessly...